Growing Up in the Delta

The Choices You Have to Make to Get Where You Want to Go

Growing Up in the Delta

The Choices You Have to Make to Get Where You Want to Go

Christine King

ISBN: 978-1-4269-4579-3 (sc)
ISBN: 978-1-4269-4799-5 (e)

Trafford rev. 12/28/2010

 www.trafford.com

North America & International
toll-free: 1 888 232 4444 (USA & Canada)
phone: 250 383 6864 ✦ fax: 812 355 4082

TABLE OF CONTENTS

To my children, grand children and great grand children

This book covers my life's journey from a small girl growing up in the Southern Delta to my adulthood, highlighting the ups and downs along the way. It is intended as a reminder, keepsake, and inspiration to my children, grand children and great grand children that they can accomplish anything in life that they want too if they are willing to work for it.

This book is about a girl growing up in the South Delta, she realizes that she does not have what it take to succeed in life. She moves from the Delta to the North where her life changed completely.

Growing Up in the Delta

This book will mostly be about my life. But I will briefly tell you about my family.

I was born and raised in the South Delta, in a small town in Mississippi, I am not the oldest. I am the sixth child; my parent had a little girl that died at an early age that was between one of my sisters and me. My parents had seven girls and two boys. Two of my sisters and my parents are now deceased. My parents, possessing neither academic honors nor financial wealth were hard workers and tried to provide what they could for our family. My father worked as a farmer and my mother as a housekeeper. We lived in a row house on a dirt road. Though kept up very good, the road was always a challenge after a heavy rain. My mother made most of our clothing. She didn't have a sewing machine; she would sew our clothing by hand. They were made from the sacks that our flour was bought in. My parents would buy flour in 25 and 50 lb sacks. The sack would have beautiful trimming around the bottom. My mother would make skirts for us from the sacks. She would take the trimming from the sacks and place it around the bottom of the skirts, and then she would wash and starch them. Our starch would be made from flour. She would then buy blouses to match the color of the trimming. We didn't have much, but my mother would make sure that we always had clean clothes to wear. She would wash them in a tin tub and scrub them on a rub board. The clothes would be hung outside to dry. We would take the clothes from the line, sprinkle with starch and iron them. Our iron was heated on a wood stove. We were all very happy, because we didn't know anything else.

But, as life would have it, when I was eight years old my mother and father separated. My mother and father had been separated before, but always going back together. But this time it was different, they didn't go back together. My mother was young when she married my father; he was eight years older. My father was married before; his first wife had passed away. When my mother would leave my father, she would always take the girls with her and my two brothers would stay with our grandfather. When my younger sisters and I were born our grandfather had passed away. My older brother told us all about our grandfather. He seemed like a very interesting person, I would have loved to been able to have spent time with him. My father's mother had also passed away before I was born. But thank God we were told all about her too. One of my cousins gave me a picture of my grandmother. When my children's and grandchildren come to visit, I tell them this is my grandmother, my father's mother. I am so proud to have a picture of her. My older brother told me that our grandmother died at an early age, and that she had died before he was born and that he only knew our grandfather on our father side. My grandmother on my mother side lived to be very old. I never knew my grandfather on my mother side, I was told about him as well. It is always good to have someone to tell you about your ancestors. I learned a lot from my cousin that live in Tennessee. He told me quite a lot about my father that I didn't' know.

In 1992, I made up my mind along with my sister that we would have a family reunion. In that way we would get a chance to meet many of our family members that we didn't know. So we did, and we have been having family reunions off and on since that time. I have met and learned about lots of my family that I didn't know before and now that we know each other we keep in touch. I Thank God for all the information I have been given. Regrettably, my father passed away before we started having family reunions.

My Older Brother Runs Away From Home

My older brother ran away from home one day. When he first ran away, he joined up with an old man selling watermelons off a truck. He had no money for almost a week; he only had watermelons to eat every day. A circus came near where he and the old man were selling watermelons from the truck. He talked with the circus manager about a job, and was hired. So, he went off with the circus and traveled from town to town. He was paid $18 a week plus board. Times were very hard for him; the circus stopped at all the towns. One day the circus was performing in a small town not far from our house, so my brother left the circus and came back home. He was home for a short while before he decided it was time for him to go on his own again.

One day my other brother got very ill. Because our local hospital was unable to care for him, he was taken to a hospital in another town; my mother had to stay with him. While he was in the hospital, we had to stay with one of our cousin and his family. My brother was in the hospital for a long time, thank God he did get better and came home and once again we were all together. My cousin is ninety-two years old now; I visited him in December of 2006. He remembered when we stayed with him and his family. He only has his younger son staying with him now. All of his other children have grown up and have families of their own. He had five children, three girls and two boys. One of his daughters also lives in Tennessee; his other three children live in other states, his wife has passed away. It is amazing how good his mind is, I hope to visit him again soon.

As time went on my two older sisters and brothers left home. They got married and had their own families. It was just my younger three sisters and me. As a result of the separation, our mother was forced to move to another town and take any work that she could find. Which normally was house cleaning, long work hours and great travel distance away from home. During those years, getting transportation was hard, sometime she would have to stay in the town where she worked for the entire week and come home only on the weekend. I was the oldest of the younger set, which were four girls. This made me responsible for the care of my three younger sisters. We lived in a two family apartment, with my Aunt Bea living next door. Aunt Bea was our Aunt's husband sister. She would look after us, but we lived in our apartment alone, until my mother came home on the weekend. We went to our Aunt Bea's apartment on Tuesday nights for prayer meetings, there we would sing and pray. Aunt Bea would play the organ and her friend would play the guitar. We were not allowed to wear pants to the prayer meeting; if we had them on we would have to change into a dress.

Our mother would come home on Saturday morning. During this time she was working and staying in Jackson, Mississippi. My sister and I would pay the bills and do our grocery shopping while my mother was home. We were the two older sisters that were still home at that time. We would walk to town, which was about one and a half miles from where we lived. Sometime on our way back home, carrying what we had purchased for our mother. The storekeeper would put our meats in brown bags, the bags would get wet and we would get home with about half of our purchase. We would be walking and playing around, not knowing our bags were losing our meats until we got home. Sometimes, we would get a ride; it would be on the back of a wagon. Our neighbors and their families would be on their ways home from doing their weekend shopping. We knew that our mother needed her rest, to be able to go back to the city on Sunday for work. We would do all that we could to help her.

Strangers Attack My Mother

My mother was robbed of her money and her life was threatened. She had cashed her check from work at a local store; a man followed her home. When she opened the door of her apartment, the man threatened her life with a large rock and took all her money. Another time my mother had a threat on her life; she was walking home from work, it was near sundown. Three men in a car asked her if she wanted a ride, she refused and kept walking. They stopped the car to make her get in, she started to run. She ran down an embankment and came out on the other side, near some houses. She screamed and knocked on someone's door; they let her in and called the police. She told us, if those three men had caught her that night and made her get into their car, she probably would be dead. My mother really did have a lot of hard times; we thank God that he kept her safe. For about a year my mother stayed in Jackson all week long and came out to the country where we were staying on weekends. She decided to move us to Jackson where she was working, so we wouldn't have to stay alone during the week and she would have us with her. The four of us girls were with our mother.

After staying in Jackson for a while, work slowed for my mother. There was a bus load of peoples going to different places to do field work. My mother and one of our aunts and her husband went along. Two cousins and my sisters and I stayed with our grandmother. Our grandmother only had one bed, so my sisters and I slept on the floor, I was nine years old. I wrote my two brothers to come and get us; they were living in the Delta. That weekend they came and got us. This was over fifty years ago, and my older brother is still living in the Delta, he comes by every week to check on my sister and me. We stayed with our brothers and their families, until our mother returned home from working in the field. Then we went back to Jackson with her. My mother was able to be home every night.

I would sometime visit, and stay with my father. I did this until I was fourteen. I would go to school from his house. After school I would carry the wood into the house, sometime I would have to churn the milk, and then I would do my homework for the next day. My father had a new family; I had a stepmother, stepsister and a stepbrother. I was not living with my mother all the time now. I was living between my older sister, brother and father house.

When I first went to live with my father, my brother and father purchased a car together, it was a 1951 Chevrolet. They would ride to work together during the week. On Saturdays one would use the car, then the other. Each one would take their family grocery shopping. I would always go to town with my brother and his wife. First, my father would use the car on Saturday morning for his shopping then he would stop by my brother's house to pick him up so he could use the car. While my father and stepmother was in town grocery shopping. My stepsister and I would be home doing the washing and cleaning. I would meet my father at the gate; he would give me my allowance for the week. My brother had two stepchildren, a girl and boy that were living with them. His wife had two more children, but they were living with some of her family. We would go to town; the three of us children would get a bag of junk food. We would get tired of eating while walking the street, and then we would sit in the car. My brother and his wife would sit in the car and talk to their friends when they came by the car, we would do this every Saturday.

My stepsister had a little girl; got married and moved out. Her and her family stayed on in the Mississippi Delta for a while, and then they moved to California. I was still staying with my father off and on. My stepbrother got married and moved away, he went to California too. Sometimes my sister and I both would stay with my father for a short time. Now, it was just my father and his wife there. I would be the one that stayed with the two of them the most. I would stay with them and go to school. Then one day I went back to stay with my mother, and I never stayed with my father again.

My brother's wife has passed away now. They were together over thirty years, and have one son. I got married a short time later and at one time lived near my father, I would see him often. We lived in a small house on the same plantation. We only lived there for a short time. I moved to the North, and would visit my father when I was down South.

One day my father got sick and had to go to the hospital, I came from the North to be with him. He had surgery; I spent the first night at the hospital with him. I slept on a small cot on the side of his bed. I stayed a few more days, and then I had to go home to go back to work. I had left my children at home with my husband. Several months later I went back to visit my father, the family went with me. My father was still sick; he wasn't getting out of bed now. He had to be taken care of; I spent the night with him. A storm came thru while he was in the hospital tearing most of the houses down, including the house where my father had been living. By the time he got out of the hospital everyone on the plantation was living in trailers. After spending the night with my father, we soon left for home again so my husband and I could go back to work, after a short time at home my father went back to the hospital. My sister was staying with him; she would call me every day to tell me how he was doing. My sister asked my father if he wanted me to come, he told her that I had little kids and I would know when to come. A couple of days later my sister was with him, she got a phone call in the hallway. She went out of the room to answer the call, when she returned to the room, my father had passed away.

My family in Mississippi called me and my family; I went to my father's funeral. I often think about him, I still miss him dearly, once while he was sick I went to visit him, he was bedridden. I kissed him on the forehead and told him that it had been a long time. He answered by telling me that it had been too long, my father lived only a few more months. I remember the day that he was buried, it was in an isolated spot; I have not been able to find his grave. His wife left the South a few days later with her son and daughter. She never came back to Mississippi; she passed away several years later.

I Meet My Husband

I met my husband who is the brother to my older sister's husband. He was visiting from a small town in Mississippi about a hundred miles away from where I lived. I was sixteen and he was nineteen when we got married. We stayed with my older sister and her family, until we were able to get a house of our own. Our first house had two rooms, a front living room that also served as a bed room and a kitchen. The house was located on a dirt road, with several other houses in a row. Some of the houses had two rooms and some had three rooms. Two of my sisters and a brother also lived in the row houses. We would walk back and forth from each other house.

My husband and I worked in the fields, chopping and picking cotton, he also drove tractors. A tractor driver got paid $7 a day. Later, they were paid $1 an hour, which amounted to $12 a day; they worked twelve hours a day. When we went to work in the fields there was a truck that picked each person up in front of their house. The driver would also return the workers to their house for lunch, and back to the field after lunch. The ladies would have two hours for lunch. During the two hour lunch break, sometimes we would have to cook, at other times we would cook ahead. The men would get one hour off for lunch. The ladies had the extra hour to cook before the men got home. It was not easy, because we were using wood stoves at the time. Later, we were able to purchase a propane stove and heater. I would work all day for three dollars, which was the wages for chopping cotton. Sometime we would work six days a week. Food was very cheap at that time; you could feed a complete family for very little money.

During the years of 1950 to 1960, I also worked as a short order cook at a Restaurant and did housekeeping. We did not own a car at that time. Some days I had to walk back and forth to work each day. I walked about a mile to get to my job as a housekeeper; I would then have to walk even farther to my second job at the restaurant. I would work both jobs, as a housekeeper during the morning and at the restaurant in the evening. At the restaurant, I would get off at 9:00 P.M.; the owner would drive me home. I was a short order cook, but when I was not doing that I would help wash the dishes. One day while washing dishes, I cut the palm of my hand very bad. All I could do was to stop working long enough to stop the bleeding, wrap my hand as tight as I could and wash the dishes with one hand. My hand did heal but it took a long time, the scar is almost invisible now.

My husband and I purchased our first car; it was a black 1949 Chevrolet; we paid $50 for it.

Our first Television (TV) was black and white; it had a coin slot where we would put in .25 cent each hour to watch it. We had the only TV in our neighborhood. The neighbors would come over and we all would put our .25 cent into the TV to watch a show. We all had very little money, on most occasions the TV would cut off when the money ran out; we would not be able to watch the entire movie. The next night the neighbors would come over again with the quarters they had. Then we would watch the TV as long as we had money to put into the TV. The TV salesman would come around once a week to collect the money from the TV. This is the way that we paid for the TV. As long as we had money for him to collect, we would be able to keep the TV. To make it color, we would use different colors of film paper. By putting it over the TV screen, we would have color. Then the family and I would gather around it. We were happy; we had color on our TV. This was before the real color TV came out.

As our lives went on; the hard work, little money and not owning much began to dominate our thoughts and conversation. My family and I started planning our great escape, leaving Mississippi, the South, for the better life in the North.

The first time we left the south, we went to Flint Michigan. We only had one child, a little girl, she was six months old. We stayed with my cousin and her family, she had two little girls. I was able to get a job at the YWCA in the kitchen. I would go shopping with the boss to purchase fruits and vegetables. My family and I stayed there for a while. During this time, my husband was not able to get steady work. This is when my little girl and I went back to the Delta. I stayed with one of my sisters and her children until my husband came back. We stayed in the Mississippi Delta for a short time, before leaving again. My younger brother and his family were now living in Missouri. He came to the Delta and got my family and me, we moved to Missouri where he was, we stayed there for several years. We found the work in Missouri was also very hard; it was as hard as living in Mississippi and in Missouri we still were not able to earn much money. We were still working in the fields and I was doing ironing by the bushel basket for the boss' wife.

Missouri is where I first started to go back to school. I knew that I needed to get more education. A friend of mine also started; along with my sister-law and her sister. The four of us went to night classes. All four of us would get together and go on Tuesday and Thursday Nights. Because we didn't have much, we would all go to the thrift shop to purchased clothes for class, and then we would go home and wash them.

I realized if I truly wanted to change my life for the better, I would have to do it myself. I always worked hard, so this would be no different. I was willing to do whatever it took to make a better life for my children. If I wanted to really change my life, I had to think positive and good things would begin happening to me. I now speak from experience; you see I got married at an early age. I was a high school dropout and had a daughter before I was eighteen years old. My husband at the time was doing all he could, I know what I was capable of doing. I had to go back to school to get a better education.

Today, I can truly say, going back to school helped me to achieve things in my life that would have been impossible. The jobs I was able to obtain and the work that I did was very important. I also got to travel to many other states as well as different countries.

The day that my second daughter was born, I had iron a bushel basket of clothes. This definitely was not going to work. This was not what we had in mind. We were doing worst instead of better. We were more tired out than before. So, we decided to leave and go someplace else. All four of our families moved from Missouri. All of us ended up in different places. My sister-law went to Illinois; her sister moved back to Mississippi, she passed away in 2009. My friend and her family moved to St. Louis, Missouri. I have never heard from them again. I moved back to Mississippi for a short time, later moving to Pennsylvania. My brother's father-law lived in Missouri; we got him to take us by car back to Mississippi.

We Move to the North

When we decided to go to Pennsylvania, we had five children three boys and two girls. The children and I stayed with my sister and her family in Mississippi until we were ready to go to Pennsylvania. My husband went ahead of us. He was able to get a job at a well-known manufacturing plant. He saved his money so that we would be able to join him. He lived with his sister and her husband.

That summer my sister -law came to Mississippi to visit her brother and my sister. When her vacation was over, we went back to the north with her. My husband had saved enough money for the apartment when we got there, and I had saved enough money working two jobs to buy our bus tickets. We boarded the bus and left, our luggage was large suitcases and cardboard boxes. When we got to Pennsylvania, we found things were different from the Mississippi Delta.

My family and I lived with my sister- law and her husband for a week, they didn't have any children. Later she and her husband adopted one of her nieces. During the first week we were looking for an apartment, we were able to find one; it was three bedrooms, living room, kitchen and bathroom, our rent was $250 a month. We went to the local thrift store to purchase what we needed. We purchased furniture for two of the bedrooms, living room, kitchen and what we needed for the bathroom. We had to leave one of the bedrooms empty until we got more money. After only a couple of weeks, we had enough money to buy furniture for the empty room. So, back to the thrift store we went, we were able to get a bed, lamp table, and something to keep our clothes in. There was another couple living up stairs, at the time, they didn't have any children, they were expecting their first. Right away the lady upstairs and I became friends. She would go with me to the thrift store, where we would find bargains. I became a member of a Baptist Church, where I was one of the clerks and press and publicity persons. I was a member there until I was transferred to my new job location in October 1995.

We were very happy; we were getting our life on track. We were truly being blessed, we had our own apartment. We also were able to buy a station wagon. We took our first trip back to Mississippi to see our family and friends. We visited with them for a week, before returning home.

My husband had been working at the plant for several years, before the plant went on strike. The plant was on strike for about six months, he was getting very little money. I knew that I would have to go to work to help with the expenses. I started to look for a job. This would be the first time that I had worked, since moving north.

My sister- law was a housekeeper at a local college. The college needed cleaning after the students had left for home over the summer break; she got me a job with her. I worked with her about a month and decided this was not what I moved to Pennsylvania to do. The work was hard and paid very little, only minimum wages. Minimum wage at that time was about $1.25 to $2.50 an hour. I got a job at a restaurant connected to a motel as a prep cook. I would prepare the salads and some of the foods for the cook. I got paid about .25 cent more an hour than I made working in housekeeping at the college, which still was very low pay.

There was more that I wanted out of life and I wanted to make my family life better too. There was a new store opening in town, I filled out an application for a job to help set up the store, I was hired. After the store was completed and ready to open, they kept me. I was trained to be manager of the children's and infants department. I was also trained as a sales clerk and cashier. This job paid a little more money an hour than my previous job. During this time, I returned to school for training to be a Certified Nurse's Aide. I finished my training and got a job at a nursing home. I worked days and later went on second shift. Every job change I would get paid a little more an hour. By working second shift, I would get paid even more an hour. One day the nursing home decided to make a pamphlet illustrating how the nursing home operated. They took a picture of me standing by a wheel chair with a patient in it; it was on the first page. I worked at the nursing home for two and a half years.

There was an opening at one of the local hospitals for a Dietary Technician. I filled an application out for the job and I was hired. I would go to the patient's room and get their menu selection for the next meal. I would read the menu selection to my tray aide; who would then fix the patients plates and put them on trays to be served. After the patients finished eating, I would then check their tray to see if my special diet patients had eaten all of their food. If they had not eaten enough, I would give them a supplemental meal. I would also order food for the entire hospital for the next day. The hospital had eight floors of patients. There was a Dietary Technician on each floor. But only one technician would order the food for all floors. I really like this job; I would meet lots of peoples.

I continued looking for a job to make more money. I worked at the hospital as a Dietary Technician for almost a year. One day I was reading the newspaper when I noticed that a manufacturing plant was hiring Spray Machine Operators. I noticed right away that I would make more money, working in a plant than working in the hospital and I wanted to be an inspector. This was my dream job, if I got the job, maybe I would get a chance too. The starting pay was $4.25 an hour. I filled the application out for the job; I was hired as a Spray Machine Operator.

When I first got hired at the plant, I would work twelve hours a day. The spray machine was in a spray booth with fixtures that had holders all around it. I would have to change the fixture to accommodate the part being spray painted. The parts would rotate around the spray booth, being sprayed on the front and back. There was a heater in the booth that would dry the parts by the time they cycled around and taken off the fixture. Sometime I would be alone operating the spray machine and sometime I had a helper to take the parts off. The operator would put the parts on the fixture, with the helper taking them off. The parts would be put into a pan to be delivered to another location in the plant. Once a month I had to clean the spray booth. I would start as soon as I got to work in the morning, usually about 7:00 A.M. I would change into overalls; drain the water from the booth, get a drum to put all the old spray paint from the booth into, scrap the walls of the booth and then clean the bottom of the booth. I would have to use a shovel to gather all the debris. Once the booth was clean and allowed to dry, I would spray paint the inside walls of the booth back to its original color white. I would fill the booth bottom back up with clean water. By then it was time to take a shower, get dress, and to go home, this was an eight-hour job. Our ladies bathroom had a shower in it; I would use it the days that I had to clean the booth. With my job as a Spray Machine Operator, I was able to buy more for my children, and we really enjoyed our life.

After about a year I got laid off, and this continued on and off until I had worked at the plant for three years. I knew that I would have to go back to school to learn even more. During the time I was laid off, I got a job cleaning offices and working at a fish plant packing fish. At the fish plant, I was on-call; they would call me when I was needed, if someone had a day off or if they just needed more help. I also went back to the local hospital part time as a Dietary Technician. I was working during the day and going to school at night, I took over 800 hours of Machining and Blue Print Reading at a vocational technical training center. By this time I was called back to work, I had learned to set-up and operate different machines. A job came available for a Drill Press Operator. I submitted an application and I got the job. For the job, I had to set-up the drill press, and read the blue print with the instructions for the particular job. There were several different set-ups, according to the part that was being machined. After working at this job for a while I got laid off again. Employees with the less seniority were always the first to get laid off.

A lady got hired about two weeks after I did in the spray machine department. We got to be very good friends and although we live in different States to this day we still are friends. We visit and keep in touch by phone. She was a helper on one of the spray machines. She also got laid off, but since she was a helper, she got called back to work before me. Later she put in for a job as a Drill Press Operate and was hired. One day while she was drilling holes in a part, an unanchored part spun around and cut her hand pretty bad. After that she applied for a job in the assembly department. She got the job, in the assembly department they would assemble and spray paint the parts.

During the time I was laid off, two of my friends who are sisters and I drove to Los Angeles California. One of the sisters from California while in Ohio purchased a car, the three of us drove the car to California. We left Ohio on Tuesday at 7:00 P.M. driving straight thru by taking turns driving. We got to Las Vegas, Nevada on Thursday evening. We stayed in Las Vegas until Saturday morning and then we drove on to Los Angeles. I stayed in Los Angeles for one week, I stayed with my stepsister. After my father passed away, my stepmother went to Los Angeles to live with her daughter and her family. Her son and daughter have grown up and have their own families; they both live in Los Angeles. My stepmother had passed away, before I went to visit.

The sister that purchased the car in Ohio lived in Los Angeles, her sister stayed in Los Angeles with her. It was a very good trip; we stopped in Arizona for souvenirs and we had a chance to do lots of sightseeing. The next Saturday, I boarded the plane for home.

A few weeks later I was called back to my Drill Press Job. Several months later they were taking applications for an Inspector. Everyone hired at this time were going to be "B" Inspectors. That meant that we were going to inspect parts that came into the shop, before the parts were machined or shipped someplace else. I filled the application out to be considered for an inspector, I was hired. I started my training; I had already taken Blue Print Reading and knew about all the inspection tools. I could also operate different machines. The job came easy for me.

After being a "B" inspector for several years. I was able to put in for an "A" Inspector. This meant I would have up to two years of training, if anytime during the training I didn't meet the training requirements; I would be dropped from the training program. I would work so many hours a day in the shop and the remaining balance of the eight hour shift in classes. We had classes inside the plant, where we would do both hands on and class room work.

I became an A-Inspector in one-and-a half years. The classes were very intense. An "A" Inspector is required to layout and check the first part that is machined before any other parts can be machined. The "A" Inspector had to know the correct inspection tools to use, there were several inspection machines that the inspector had to be able to operate and the inspector had to ensure that the part was laid out correctly to the blue print.

Once there was an instructor that had been hired to come into the plant to teach the classes, told me that I did not have the background to be an "A" Inspector. I loved the job; my background was perfect for this job. I was proud that I proved the instructor wrong; I just had to be willing to learn. When the instructor made the remark to me, I knew that I would have to do better than he expected me too. I went on to be an Inspector for twenty years. I only wish that the instructor that tried to keep me from improving myself, by trying to give me doubts knew that I successfully made it as an "A" Inspector. What he didn't know was that God was on my side.

While working there, I met some very nice people. We would get together outside of work. Some of them have passed away now, and the others are still friends. I keep in touch with them by phone and sometimes card at special occasions. These friends would sometime surprise me by stopping by my house with donuts and I would make coffee for us, we would sit around talking for hours. I was invited to their homes, where we would have a pool parties.

Big Changes in the Delta

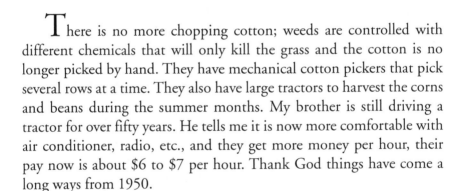

There is no more chopping cotton; weeds are controlled with different chemicals that will only kill the grass and the cotton is no longer picked by hand. They have mechanical cotton pickers that pick several rows at a time. They also have large tractors to harvest the corns and beans during the summer months. My brother is still driving a tractor for over fifty years. He tells me it is now more comfortable with air conditioner, radio, etc., and they get more money per hour, their pay now is about $6 to $7 per hour. Thank God things have come a long ways from 1950.

Almost everyone that lived in the Delta on plantations has moved away from the farms into the inner cities and from the modest shacks to purchased homes. In 1950, my two brothers and older sisters lived on a plantation.

Today, none of my family is on plantations. They are living in the city, or have moved to the north. My oldest brother still lives in the Mississippi Delta; he is eighty-three years old now and still drives a tractor and works full time. After many years in the south, my youngest brother moved to the north, my two older sisters have passed away. As a child, my younger three sisters and I sometimes stayed with them and their families when our mother was away working.

We Purchase a House

We rented our first apartment for seventeen months, and then we were able to purchase a house. It was a large two-story house on a very quiet street. The house had two apartments; on the first floor there were three bedrooms, living room, kitchen, bathroom and a basement. The second floor had three bedrooms, living room, kitchen, bathroom and an attic. The house had a porch upstairs and down stairs.

By this time, I had six children, three boys and three girls; it was time for me to really get serious about going back to school. I started school by going at night. I went back to get the education that I always wanted to better myself. My sister worked at the Nursing Home as a Certified Nurse's Aide; she worked the night shift for seven years.

My sister lived upstairs with her son, and my family and I lived downstairs. She lived upstairs for several years and then she moved to a house not far from us. Once my sister moved, we opened up the house so that we could go from downstairs to the upstairs without going outside. My oldest son was now married and had a family. He also was in the military and had to go overseas, so his family moved upstairs. They stayed upstairs until he returned to the United States and then they moved to Alabama.

My husband and I were now divorced. My older son and daughter had families of their own. I had brought a house, this time by myself. My youngest son was living with his father, and one son and my two youngest daughters were living with me. My two younger sons were also in the National Guard. My son that was living with his father had left his father and was living with me again and my next to older son was now living in the house that my ex-husband and I purchased.

I left Pennsylvania to go on vacation in the South, when I arrived at my sister's house, she ran out to the car to tell me that the house my son was living in had been destroyed by fire. My son was in the house at the time. Thank God the next-door neighbor woke him up.

When I returned to Pennsylvania, I found the house a total loss, there was nothing left but part of the foundation. Everything in the house got burned up including a car in the driveway that was burned. This is when my next to older son came back to live with me. He lived with me until my job transferred me to my new location.

My youngest daughter got married and moved to the state of Washington with her husband, he was in the military at that time. They were there for several years, and then they came back to Pennsylvania.

I was able to visit them in Seattle Washington twice, each visit lasting for a week. I would fly into Tacoma /Seattle Airport. The first visit my daughter was expecting her first child, the second visit was when the child was born, she had a son. The weather in Washington was different from Pennsylvania, it would rain in the morning and the sun would come out in the afternoon. Seattle was a lovely place. My daughter and I would take the bus to the Military Base, where we did our shopping. Since my daughter no longer lives in Seattle, I probably will not get a chance to visit there again. After returning home I went back to work. My youngest daughter has three boys now. She and her husband are no longer together.

Of my mother's six girls and two boys, my two younger sisters were in Pennsylvania. My youngest sister got married and moved to Illinois, later she returned to the south and then she came to Pennsylvania to live. My other sister had gotten married and moved to Tennessee. She would leave Tennessee and move to Illinois. She didn't like Illinois and moved to Pennsylvania too. Then because of the brutal Pennsylvania winters, one day she decided to move to a warmer climate, she wanted to get out of the cold and snow. She and her family left Pennsylvania and moved to Alabama, where my oldest son was living, she is now very happy.

My mother and my youngest brothers also moved to Pennsylvania. Three of my sisters and one of my brothers choose to stay in the South. They would visit us in Pennsylvania, but they always returned to the South. My two older sisters have now passed away. My youngest sister and her family still live in Pennsylvania, along with my youngest brother and his family.

The Day I Submit Application for Government Job

O ne day while I was working, a Government Inspector Supervisor had notice that every time he came in to visit his Government Inspectors that were station at the plant, he would see me working.

So, he had one of his Inspectors ask me if I would consider filling out an application to be a Government Inspector. I did, and after almost a year I had forgotten that I had filled out an application. I had a good job that I enjoyed. The Government Inspector came out into the plant to tell me that I had a call in his Office. When I went to answer the phone, it was the Government Inspector's Supervisor on the phone. He told me that if I was still interested in a job, that I was hired. I was so happy; I put in my two weeks' notice that day, I was working afternoon shift. My co-workers were very happy for me, but surprised.

My friend that I had met two weeks after I started to work at this manufacturing plant as a Spray Machine Operator Aide, she was still working at the plant. She worked there for several more years after I left. Then there was a layoff, the peoples that got laid off at this time, most of them wouldn't be going back, she was one of them. I had been a "B" Inspector, an "A" Inspector, and now I was getting the chance to be a Government Inspector. God was truly working in my life. If I had still been working at the plant, I probably would have been laid off too. I had been a "B" and "A" Inspector for ten year from 1979 to 1989.

Early Monday morning two weeks later, I was in the Government office in another town. Filling out papers and getting my job assignment to work in my own home town. I was not able to be a Government Inspector in the manufacturing plant where I worked. I was assigned to a different plant. The plant that I was assigned to was a part of the plant that my ex-husband worked in. I would go to the area that he worked in to inspect parts from his co-workers. But I didn't have to inspect the work that he did, he was a Grip Blast Operator. There was another guy who was hired the same day as me. Bob was assigned to the plant that I once was an inspector at. Since I had been a "B" and an "A" inspector at the plant, I was not allowed to work there.

Now, the training really got started, we traveled to different cities and took so many classes. Bob and I would always travel together. Some of our classes were at colleges and so many of them in class room setting. I even went back to school on my own at night and took even more classes. I took four parts of engineering classes and a class in auditing on my own to better myself even more. All of my engineering and audit classes were taken at Behrend College. Some of my classes required travel to different states, and range from one to four weeks straight. We would have a test every Friday, and I would have to make above eighty percent score to pass. Some of our classes were very difficult; I would have to study really hard. I thank God that I was able to pass all of my classes. As long as I was working for the government, the job required continues training and refresher classes on a regular basis.

My Transfer to New Job Location

My job transferred me to another city, where I had to change job classification for a couple of years. My transfer location was three and a half hours drive from my home. My next to oldest son lived with me, didn't move with me when I got the transfer. He stayed on in our hometown; he now has a family of his own. Bob the guy that got hired the same day as I was as a Government Inspector, he got transferred to North Carolina. Bob sold his home and his family moved to North Carolina. I was able to keep my house since my transfer was closer.

I travel to my new work location one weekend to check the hotels out and look around for a place to stay. This was a place that I had never been too, I didn't know anyone there. I stayed at a motel close to work for the first six weeks, until I could find someplace else to live. I literally could see the building where I worked from the hotel. Our office was on the second floor. Downstairs from the office was a restaurant; I would buy my lunch there. On my way back to the motel after work I would stop by and get my dinner. There was always a pot of coffee downstairs in the motel, I would stop on my way to the room and get a cup to go with my dinner. There was a mall across the street, on Saturdays I would go there, and just walk around. Then I would go back to the room and watch TV.

It was after midnight on the first day that I had gotten to my new location when I received a call from my sister that my mother had passed away. When the midnight nurses went in to check on her, she had passed away, she died in her sleep.

My mother was in a nursing home. Before she went to the nursing home, she was staying with my sister and her family during the week. Because I worked during the week, on weekends I would pick my mother up at my sister's house and she would stay with me over the weekend. My mother lived with my sister and her family for several years before going into the nursing home. My sister was unable to keep her any longer. My mother would wonder out of the house and go walking down the street. Sometime she didn't know where she was going, we were afraid that she might get hurt. Friends and neighbors would see her and give her a ride back home. After repeated incidents, reluctantly we took my mother to a nursing home for her to look around.

My mother like the nursing home, and told us that she wanted to live there. She enjoyed helping the nurses; she would fold towels for them. There was one patient there that adored my mother. He was bedridden; my mother would pull the cover up for him and just sit and talk to him. When he saw her walking into the room he would just smile. When my mother first went to the nursing home, she was on the first floor. One day they went in to check on her and she had left the nursing home, she went for a walk down the street. She had no idea where she was going, they went and found her. After that, she was moved to the second floor. There was an alarm on the back door upstairs. If any of the patients would open the back door to go out, the alarm would go off; alerting the nurses to check the door.

My mother got sick and stopped eating. She had to be admitted to the hospital for a feeding tube. While she was in the hospital, she got pneumonia; this was the first time that my mother had ever been in a hospital in her life. She quickly got better and was out of the hospital and back at the nursing home. I would visit her every day after work and take care of her hair. There was a room in the nursing home that was used as a beauty shop. A beautician came into the nursing home once a week to do some of the ladies hair. I would take care of my mother's hair; I would wash and curl her hair. I would also give her a bath or shower. I would tell her "You took care of me, and now I am taking care of you", she would just smile. Every evening I would take her a snack. She loved to eat snacks in the evening after dinner. She loved bananas, I would stop at the store on my way to the nursing home to get bananas for her, every evening we would take a walk down the hall, after the walk I would put her to bed before going home.

My mother had been at the nursing home for some time before my job transfer. My only regret to the transfer and move to my new location was that I had to leave my mother. Transferring was the only way that I could keep my job. I visited her the Saturday prior to leaving. I called my sister at the nursing home on Sunday and Monday evening. My mother passed away Monday night. She would no longer be at the nursing home for me to call or to visit.

On October 24, 1995, my mother passed away, she was eighty-seven years old. She had been at the nursing home for 2 years. Now, I had to make the trip back home by myself, something that I had never done. Two days earlier two of my sons had traveled with me to my new location. My oldest son was in the Military and stationed in Virginia did the driving for me. My youngest son was living with him. They were back in Virginia; they had made sure that I arrived at my new location safely.

Now, I had to go back home alone. I made the trip by myself, I got lost once. There was a man at a store that got me back on the right track. My sister told me on the phone to be at her house by 12:00 noon. We would have to make arrangements for my mother's funeral. By the grace of God, I arrived at her house at 11:45 A.M. I was so upset; I parked on the wrong side of the street. When I went back out to my car ten minutes later to get some earrings that we were going to put on my mother, I had a parking ticket. This was the only parking ticket that I had gotten in my entire life, it was $15. Of all days to get a ticket, on the day that I was making my mother's funeral arrangement. I paid the ticket before I left to go back to my new location. We made the arrangements, and called all of the family with the details. The funeral was later that week; God was with me all the way.

I was away from my new job for a week. When I returned, I started looking for an apartment. I found one in no time. I had to wait until it came available for me to move in. It was in a large brick building, which had four efficiency apartments. The rent was $225 a month. I had a kitchen with a section for a small table with two chairs, a bedroom large enough for a small section for the living room and a bathroom. I would have to walk down a long hallway to get to my apartment. College students rented the other three apartments.

I met a lady; her family had been transferred to this town with her job, she worked for a different company. Her family had been in the town long enough to learn where the churches were located. She picked me up the first Sunday that I arrived back in town from my mother's funeral. I was staying at the motel. I went to church with her, and that Sunday I became a member. She would pick me up for church every Sunday after that, until I learned my way around. I sang with the senior choir. I also was treasure for the choir. There was a senior, adult, men and children's choir, our senior choir song on the first and third Sunday. The adult choir would sing on fourth Sunday the children choir would sing on the second Sunday. The men choir would always sing on the fifth Sunday. Our choirs traveled a lot, we went on near and far trips. We would go to the local cable station a week or two before Christmas to do taping for our Christmas Program. The ladies would all wear a black skirt and red top. The program could be watched on TV a few days before Christmas.

After leaving the motel, I lived in the efficiency apartment for six months. Then I was able to get a two-bedroom townhouse. It had a living room, kitchen, bathroom and a patio on the back. There was a large picture window on the front and back of the apartment. The rent was $300 a month. The apartment was all-electric, so you had to pay the electric bill. The water and sewage was included in the rent. I stayed in the townhouse for ten months. I paid rent according to what I got paid. By the time I moved, my rent was $310. During this time, my job required me to travel from plant to plant and I continued to take classes.

After being in my new location almost a year and half, one of my friends called to tell me that one of my friends that I worked with at the nursing home had passed away, she would ride to work with me. She was a mother at her church.

I started to check the newspaper and magazines on houses for sale. I visited several houses before I found the one that I wanted. I went by the realtor office one day after work; to see the houses, they had pictures of it on their board. There was this red and white house on a hill on the board. One of the realtor agents spoke up and said to me this is the house for you, I told him that I was new in town and that I had no idea where the street was located. The next day I was off work, so the agent and I took a drive to the house. It was only about twenty minutes from where I worked. I fell in love with the house at first sight. I made a bid for the house right then. The agent told me that the owner was out of town. He would be back on Monday, this was Thursday. The agent called me on Monday at work and told me that the owner accepted my bid. It was his mother's house, she had passed away, and he was an only child.

I would have a nice large garden, already fenced in. I would be able to plant all kind of vegetables. I would share them with my friends and neighbor. The yard was very nice, good grade of grass, flat and easy to care for. The owner even gave me a riding lawn mower. This was perfect, since I would be taking care of the lawn and grass mostly by myself. I also had a big flood light on the back of the house. It would automatically come on from sun down until sun up. The house had a brick front and aluminum siding on the sides and back. It was in a nice location; near a shopping mall, fast food restaurants, dry cleaner, drug store, movie theatre, hardware store and a store where you could rent movies, all within walking distance. The house had three bedrooms, living room, dining room, kitchen and one bathroom. There was a large deck when you went out the back door. The garage was under the house; I also had a full basement with a washroom. In the eight years that I lived in the house; I added a bathroom with a shower in the basement, I did some landscaping in the front yard, enlarged the walkway and stairs with red pavers and had a two-car carport installed.

My stepbrother that lived in Los Angeles had passed away by now. He was a preacher and had his own church. I got a chance to visit him in Los Angeles twice before he passed away. My first visit was when my friends and I drove to Los Angeles. I had not seen my stepbrother and stepsister since my father passed away. That had been twenty years ago. We were very glad to see each other, and thanks to God, I was able to surprise my stepbrother by going to his church that Sunday morning with his sister. She had not told him that I was in town. He saw me from the pulpit, and said thank God; this is my sister that I have not seen for twenty years.

After church my stepbrother, his wife, my stepsister, and I went out to dinner. We talked about old times and got reacquainted with each other. I am thankful to God that we got a chance to do this before he passed away. My stepsister got a friend of her family to take us to Hollywood the next day. We did some sightseeing and shopping, we also had lunch. I really did enjoy this time with my stepsister and stepbrother's family. When I visited my stepsister and her brother for the second time, I learned from my stepbrother, that one of his daughters had passed away.

My Granddaughter is Killed

At the time, I was living at the new location when it happened. My sister called me to tell me that something had happen at my daughter's house. This message was on my answering machine when I returned home from choir practice. I called her right away, not knowing what had happen. She told me that my granddaughter had been killed.

On August 5, 1999, two weeks prior to her sixteenth birthday, my daughter's oldest child was killed; her little girl was taken from her. My granddaughter was killed by a seventeen year old boy while she was sitting on her living room sofa. Since we truly believe in God, we know it was his will. But, we missed her dearly and always will.

I called my older son who resided in Virginia; he had already got a call from his cousin. He told me to stay at home, that he and his family would be coming by later that night; they came by and spent the night. Early the next morning, we left to go to my daughter's house. Her and her family was living in the house that I lived in before I was transferred to my new location. When we got to the house, they already had the young man in police custody.

The seventeen-year-old boy received the punishment of twenty years minimum to forty years maximum. He is eligible for parole in twenty years; he will be thirty-eight years old. My granddaughter will never walk this earth again; we will never hear her voice, see her smile or laugh. We pray for God to continue to give us strength to be able to endure.

On August 5, 2008, my granddaughter had been dead for nine years. On August 24, 2008, she would have celebrated her twenty-fifth birthday. My daughter had three girls; she was the oldest, now she has two. Her youngest daughter is now in her senior year of high school, the next to the oldest is in her last year of college.

Our lives were changed forever. All of my six children's have grownup and have families. Even my youngest son has his own family; he has a boy and a girl. His daughter now has two children, a boy and girl. My next to older son and younger daughter were the last one living with me. They are now on their own and have families. My ex-husband went on disability and retired from the plant. He was living with his sister, before he moved to Michigan and remarried, his second wife passed away last year. His sister's husband also passed away. The child that they adopted; her niece's daughters, has grown up and has her own family, she lives in North Carolina.

My Trip to South Africa

At work, I was still traveling and taking classes; sometimes as long as a month at one time. I had been an inspector for the government for ten years and an inspector for a contractor for ten years, twenty years of my life had been as an inspector, I decided to retire.

On December 31, 2000, I took an early retirement. The first thing I wanted to do after retiring was to travel. I was told about a trip to South Africa, I had always wanted to visit there. So, right away I said that I would love to go.

On March 6, 2001, we left for South Africa. We went by car from Pennsylvania to Washington, DC. There we met up with forty-four people from different parts of the country; Arizona, California, the District of Columbia, Georgia, Nebraska, New Jersey, Maryland, Ohio, Pennsylvania, Oregon, and Virginia.

We boarded a plane to London England, when we arrived in London, where we were met and escorted to a luxury coach; I got a chance to go on a sightseeing tour. We visited the Tower of London, Westminster Abbey, and the British National Museum. We did some shopping and had lunch at a restaurant. That afternoon we boarded the plane for Johannesburg, South Africa where we were met by the travel representative.

After clearing customs and immigration, our luggage was loaded on the coach. We were able to go to the bank in the airport to exchange our traveler's cheques into Rands. Rand rates went up and down, during the time we were in South Africa. For $100 in U.S. currency, we got $764.53 in Rands. We travel by luxury coach for a brief city orientation tour of Johannesburg as we made our way to our first hotel, Shumba Valley Lodge, where we spent our first evening. The lodge was twenty minutes from Johannesburg.

Once checked into the hotel, freshened up and had a light lunch, we left by coach for a guided tour of Gold Reef City, which was a re-creation of old time "Johannesburg". Johannesburg came into its own as a major city when gold was discovered there in 1886. Gold Reef City is a recreational park with many activities including Siyagida Africa Dancing. You could see how they melt gold and if you were willing to wear a hardhat, rain slicker and go down in a mineshaft to actually see how gold was mined in the early years.

When we went back to the hotel, a barbeque dinner was served, followed by traditional African Dancing and entertainment. We had an information brief and a get acquainted session with the fellow travelers. We were paired two to a room; if you were traveling along, they tried to pair you with someone with a similar disposition. My roommate was a retired school teacher from Pennsylvania. We got along good; every night at dinner we would have a glass of red wine, and later that night we would have a cup of tea. It has been five years since our trip; we still keep in touch by cards or phone.

The next morning we had a buffet breakfast; it was our first breakfast in South Africa. After breakfast, we checked out of the hotel and boarded the coach to Sun City in the North Province; the trip was one and a half hour drive. Before arriving in Sun City, we went to the small town of Rustenburg where we were introduced to the people of the Royal Bafokeng. These Setswana peoples owned the land which contains the richest deposit of platinum in Southern Africa. After our visit, we boarded the coach for the remaining trip to Sun City.

Our group was hosted at a buffet lunch on the pool deck of the magnificent palace of the Lost City; this was a very beautiful place. The weather was hot; we were all given washcloths rollup with ice inside. We would use the towel to dap our face and neck. After lunch the group met for transfer to the Sun City Cabanas. The hotel was set like a jewel in the scenic splendor of the Pilansberg.

Later, that day we met outside the hotel and were taken on a game drive in open land rovers, through the Pilansberg game reserve. There were many animals in the game reserve, Elephants, Lions, Buffalos, Rhinos, Snakes, Leopards, and Baboons. It started to rain while we were on the game reserve; we were all given rain ponchos.

That evening we returned back to the hotel, we were greeted with juice in long stem glasses, we had dinner at the Calabash Restaurant. We stayed overnight at the Cabanas Hotel. After a very early buffet breakfast in the Palm Terrace the next morning we departed. We boarded a coach and were taken on a guided tour of South Africa Administrative Capital, Pretoria. We visited Voortrekker Monument, the Union Building and the U.S. Embassy. We then went to the Train Restaurant midway between Johannesburg and Pretoria for lunch. The train called the old Blue Train, served 140 Exotic South African Dishes. Believe it or not, the Blue Train is a luxury you can afford. The Train Restaurant in Midrand is a unique restaurant by world standards, consisting of four perfectly restored railway carriages, which in 1920 was used to form part of the Blue Train. Four separate dining cars decorated in an Edwardian style comfortably seat up to 176 people and there is a separate dining room that will accommodate up to 180 guests for larger functions such as wedding and parties. The food was as unique as the setting; there were enticing arrays of imaginative and unusual dishes. The entrees included salads, soups; seafood, an unusual variety of delicacy such as smoked Buffalo, Wart Hog, Zebra in bean sauce, tail of Crocodile in mushroom or litchi, Game Pie, Guinea Fowl, fried worms or Rabbit Stew are some of the more exciting options. For those who are less adventurous, there was a wide selection of traditional foods such as Lamb Chops, Steaks, Curries, Ham and Fish. The dessert table was a mouthwatering display which included all the favorites such as Chocolate Mousse, Trifle, Jelly, Ice Cream, Custard, Fruit Tart and Baked Alaska, just to name a few. The entire feast was reasonably priced making the Train an affordable and enjoyable outing.

After lunch we travel to the Museum Africa where we were taken on a fascinating guided tour, which included a lecture on Nelson Mandela famous Rivonia Trial. In 1956, 156 peoples were accused of high treason and prosecuted in a trial that lasted four years. The trial was the turning point in the consolidation of apartheid and of resistance to it. This was followed by a forty five minute tour of the early years of Johannesburg, including, how the mineworkers influenced the community, the slum yards and Sophia Town Shebeen. Then we departed for Lesedi Cultural Village. This was a multicultural Africa Village set among the pristine Bushveld and Rocky Hills of the Magaliesburg mountain range. Situated at Lesedi are a number of different traditional homesteads. The Xhosa had beautiful thatched homes and red blankets. The Zula showed us their fighting shields and cozy beehive huts. The Nebula had colorful murals. The Pedi courtyards and rhythmic drum, and the conical straw hats and sturdy mountain ponies of the Basotho. We shared a truly stirring and unique experience with the African families.

Dinner was served at the BOMA Restaurant where we were entertained by the people of the village with traditional dances and stories that date back to the days of their ancestors. Our group was able to dance with them. We then returned to the Holiday Inn Garden Court Sandton City. This hotel was located in the heart of Johannesburg Northern Suburbs. The hotel forms part of Sandton City, Africa's second largest shopping mall, we stayed overnight at the hotel.

After a buffet breakfast at the hotel, the coach departed for a full day tour of Soweto. We then were shown a cross section of life in South Africa largest city. Soweto, a sprawling metropolis of more than 3.5 million peoples on the outskirts of Johannesburg, today it is a multi-cultural composite of South Africa. Our first stop was at the Wesley Methodist Church in Dube where we attended the morning service. Visiting the Wesley Methodist Church was a memorable experience. The sermon was delivered in three languages, hearing the choir sing so harmoniously without any kind of instrumental accompaniment, and meeting the warm and wonderful people of the church. Several people from my group sang along, including me. The song we sang was "Soon and very soon". Then we all sang the song "Amen and I Adore Him". After church we carried on with our tour of the black township. We visited Freedom Square and stood on the only road in the world, which has the honor of two recipients of the Nobel Peace Prize, Nelson Mandela and Desmond Tutu.

We saw Southern Africa largest hospital. We passed by the homes of the rich and famous as well as informal settlements. We visited Wandy Tavern, one of Soweto famous Shabeens where the local congregate. After lunch we continued our tour of Soweto. We visited the Orlando Children Home, where all of us took gifts for the small babies and children to age eighteen. Our gifts consisted of socks, tee-shirts, underclothes, baby's outfits and diapers.

The next morning after a buffet breakfast we checked out of the hotel. We then went to the University of Witwatersrand where a senior faculty member on education in the New South Africa addressed us; he spoke of the transformation that had taken place in the country. After the presentation, we took a short tour of the University.

We then boarded the coach for Johannesburg International Airport for our flight to Durban; lunch was served on the plane. When we arrived in Durban, a luxury coach was waiting for us. We were taken on a tour of Durban; we then had a chance to change our traveler cheques into Rand before being taken to our hotel. We stayed at the Holiday Inn Garden Court Marine Parade; we had a spectacular view overlooking the Indian Ocean.

In front of the hotel are curio stalls which stock beadwork and crafts made by the local black community. After check in, we went shopping at the stalls across the street. That afternoon we all met in Saagries Restaurant located in the hotel, where typical Indian cuisine was served. We stayed overnight at the hotel. The next morning we had a buffet breakfast at the hotel, we boarded the coach for a full day guided tour of Durban, which included a visit to one of Durban main township areas, where we visited a children's Lutheran school in the area, the Christianenberg Primary School. We all took gifts; computer paper, crayons, writing materials etc. seeing the young children struggling against the adversity of poverty is truly a moving experience and hearing these children sing will surely touch your heart.

After leaving the Lutheran school, we were given a city tour, passed South Africa's largest hostel which houses 20,000 people. The City Tour included a stop at the Durban Africa Art Centre. The Durban African Art Centre is unique in South Africa, as an outlet it has a wide range of creative works, including beadwork, baskets, ceramics, fabrics, woodcarving, weaving and fine art. The Durban Africa Art Centre is a non-profit development project that began in 1960 and is bursting with original works at prices ranging from 3 to 3,000 Rand (US 0.40 to US $400). We then stopped for lunch and went to the Victoria Flea Market, which is the largest Indian Flea Market in the Southern Hemisphere. Afterwards we boarded the coach to return to the hotel, we had dinner and stayed overnight.

The next morning we had an early buffet breakfast at the hotel, checked out and boarded the coach. We were on our way to Durban International Airport for our flight to Cape Town. We had a light snack on the plane. When we arrived in Cape Town there was a luxury coach waiting for us. We then took a Cape Town city orientation tour that included a drive through District Six, the Malay Quarter, and Signal Hill, which overlooks Cape Town. The weather was good so we got a chance to ride the cable car, which whisks you to the top of Table Mountain in four minutes. The frequency of the Cable Car is totally dictated by the weather conditions. At the top of Table Mountain, you could see forever, with a 360 degree view of all that the Fairest Cape has to offer. We were able to buy souvenirs and cards on Table Mountain.

We returned back to the hotel, had dinner, the rest of the evening we were on our own. After breakfast the next morning, we departed on a tour of Cape Peninsula, along one of South Africa most scenic and popular routes. The tour initially flanks the colder Atlantic Ocean route to Hout Bay, once a fishing community, now one of the most popular residential areas, the harbor still has a charm of the days gone by. The tour continued over the famous Chapman's peak, there was a 200 meter drop on one side of the coach and a 200 meter rise on the other, as we made our way South, following the Atlantic Ocean until we reached Cape Point and the Cape of Good Hope. Said to be the romantic meeting place of the two mighty oceans, the Atlantic and the Indian. We then started winding our way back to Cape Town through the impressive mountains that surround the city.

We stopped at the famous Groot Constantia Wine Farm, against a backdrop of the majestic Table Mountain. We enjoyed the renowned Chardonnays, Blancs and Steins of the sought after Cape wine lands not to mention the rich, full bodied Cabernets and Shiraz. We all sampled the different wines. Some in our group purchased wine to carry home. We boarded the coach to return to the hotel, where we freshened up for dinner. We then went to an Africa Café; that was a popular local restaurant, which offers a bottomless buffet of sixteen types of typically South African food. Some of us wore African Attire that we had purchased earlier. After we had eaten, we returned to the hotel for the night.

The next morning after breakfast, we took the short walk to St. George Cathedrals where Desmond Tutu served as Archbishop of the Anglican Church until 1996 when he retired; we were given a tour of the church. This Church is the seat of the leading cleric for the Anglican Church. Then we got a guided tour of the South African Parliament. There are two houses of Parliament; first we visited the National Assembly, Visitors Gallery. There were lots of seats for the National Assembly Members of Parliament, voted for in the election. We were told that the President sits to the right of the Speaker. The press sits in the press gallery and report on proceedings. The Speaker is the Chairperson of the National Assembly. The other house of Parliament is the National Council of Provinces. This is the oldest part of Parliament. All nine Provinces are represented in National Council of Provinces, local government is also represented. Together, the National Assembly and the National Council of Provinces work to develop laws for the country. The old British coat of arms, this part of Parliament was built in the days of Queen Victoria when the Cape was a British Colony. The President is elected by Parliament. Every year the President makes a major speech in Parliament, but he does not have the right to vote in the house. There are many important women in Parliament. Their job is to keep order in the National Assembly, chair the meetings and give everybody a fair chance to speak.

Next, we went to the Victoria and Alfred Waterfront for lunch. After lunch we proceed to Berties Landing at the docks for our boat ride to Robben Island. Robben Island is where the prison was located where Nelson Mandela was held. We were given a guided tour of the Island, visited the prison, Nelson Mandela's home, for eighteen years. At the prison we photographed Mandela's tiny cell, his recreation room, his meal hall etc. We also took a tour down to the quarry where Mandela was forced to spend hours and hours breaking rocks. Our guides on the island were former inmates, who as political prisoners also spent time at the infamous facility. We then returned by boat to where the coach was waiting for us. We returned to the hotel, had dinner, and stayed the night.

The next day was our final day in South Africa; we had set the day aside for our final shopping. After breakfast we headed for Green Market Square Flea Market that was about two minutes walk from the hotel. There are always lots of flea markets to go too. There were several located in the center of down town Cape Town. Afterwards, we packed everything and changed all of our Rand back into U.S. dollars.

The next morning we had breakfast early. The coach picked us up at 5:00 A.M. to take us to Cape Town International Airport for our return flight. Before we left, we were able to take all of our VAT (value-added-tax) original invoice vouchers as well as the actual purchases to the merchant redeem center, we got all of our taxes refunded. Since we didn't live there our tax money was given back to us. There was a place at the Airport for this. We were flown to London then we changed planes to Washington, DC.

There were three of us ladies from my hometown that went to South Africa. One of the lady's husbands had taken us to Washington by car, so that we could meet up with the other tour groups. When we returned to Washington, my friend's husband picked us up at the Washington Airport to take us back to Pennsylvania by car. I enjoyed and experienced a fantastic trip. This was one trip that I will never forget.

Home from South Africa

After our trip, the three of us ladies would gather to celebrate our birthday together. We would go to a buffet restaurant; two of us would pay for the birthday girl's dinner and we would get together for parties and community gatherings. I traveled with them to the Baptist Convention and we would go shopping and just have fun, we really enjoyed it.

In June 2001, those of us who took the trip to South Africa were invited to a reception in honor of her majesty, Dr. Semane Bonolo Molotlegi, Queen Mother of the Royal Bafokeng Nation. The ladies from my town that had travel to South Africa drove to the reception held for Queen Mother of the Royal Bafokeng Nation while she was visiting the College in Pittsburg Pennsylvania. It was a very enjoyable event, and it was good to see the Queen Mother again, we saw her while in Africa. In addition to the wonderful reception, we were served a fine meal. Our Menu consisted of a basket of fresh greens, roasted Roma Tomatoes with Buffalo Mozzarella in assorted infused oils, Potato Crusted Rack of Lamb, Risotto Milanese, Fresh Steamed Asparagus with Shallot Butter, Meringue Swans filled with fresh berries and Sabayon Sauce. This was the last time that the three of us traveled together.

One year later, one of the ladies, my friend, passed away. The lady that husband had driven us to Washington got sick; a few hours later she passed away. I will always remember the trip to Africa, the reception and our friendship.

It is time for me to go back to my volunteering. I was the treasurer for our local NAACP Chapter for two years and I was their press and publicity spokesman for four years. As the treasurer, I would keep track and report all their financial transactions, the income and outgoing. As the press and publicity spokesperson I would ensure that anything that had to be reported got to the local newspaper or media. I also operated the video camera when we did our monthly videotaping. We would interview peoples from throughout the community on varies topics. I was one of the directors during the videotaping, I would tell the interviewer how many minutes were remaining and when to wrap up the program.

I also volunteered at one of the local hospitals in town. It kept me busy; I was retired and wanted to keep busy. I volunteered on Tuesdays and Fridays. I got lots of enjoyment from volunteering. It made me happy knowing that I was helping others. As a volunteer at the hospital, I worked with two other volunteers. During the Christmas holiday we would wear a Santa Cap. It would make the patients smiles when they saw us with our caps on. I remember, two days before Christmas a patient walked into the hospital as I was greeting patients at the door. He passed me a small napkin; inside the napkin was the most beautiful angel, he had made it. He told me that this angel reminded him of me, helping everyone with a smile. I really did enjoy volunteering.

Back to the Delta

The day that I decided to move back south, was a very snowy, cold day. I had been out shoveling snow since 5:00 A.M. in the morning and my wrist was hurting. When I went inside the house, I called my sister in Mississippi, I told her that if she could find me a house to buy that I would move back to Mississippi, she didn't believe me, but she did what I asked.

She had seen a for sale sign on a mailbox in front of a very nice house nearby. She got the number off the mailbox on her way to school to pick up her grandchildren. She called me and gave the number to me. I called the owner that same night. The owner seemed very nice, after talking he agreed to take his for sale sign down that night. I told him that I would send a deposit check the next day, that way he would know that I was serious about buying the house. I asked the owner could my sister and niece look inside the house, he said that they could that night. After my sister and niece saw the house, they called me and told me that the house was nice; they knew that I would make changes to suit my liking. God was working in this plan, the owner trusted me to buy his house without seeing me in person. I mailed the deposit the next day. This was a God sent for me, I would be able to get a house and move before the next winter. Two weeks later I went south and purchased the house. It had three bedrooms, two full bathrooms, living room, dining room, kitchen and a screen in back porch.

I put the house that I had purchased at my new location up for sale. It was going to be my retirement house; I had remodeled it to my liking. My house was sold in three weeks. It was time to change my mind about living in the North. My youngest son had moved to be near me. Now, I was getting ready to move south. He prepared to move back to our hometown. There he would be near his sisters and brother. Five of my six children live in the town. I am not near them, but they are near each other, I thank God for that. They know that they are only a phone call away from their older brother and me.

It was now time for me to start making arrangements to move back South.

In May, I packed up everything with the help of my friends and three sons. Because of the amount of furniture and other belongings that I had accumulated between the two homes, we had to make two trips. My oldest son drove the truck on the first trip. He came from Virginia to help me move. My younger son drove the truck on my second trip with my middle son, traveling with him, they both live in Pennsylvania. My sons rode in the moving truck, while my friend and I were in the car. The move and the ride were very hard on all of us, since we were traveling so far over two weekends. We stopped only long enough to offload the first truck load, get one night of sleep and then return to Pennsylvania to pick up the final load.

I was moving back to a place that I had left when I was very young. My house was sold by now. My son had moved back to our hometown in Pennsylvania and I was ready to settle in the South once again. I have learned to appreciate the fact, that my moving from the South really did change my life and that moving back after retirement was okay. Especially, since I had earned a living and didn't have to look for work. My childhood home town is small, there is some work in town, but the jobs are already filled. Most of the people here have to travel to nearby larger towns to get jobs. The commute is not so hard on the younger people. But peoples my age would not want to have to travel every day, winter and summer or in the harsh weather.

To occupy my time and to fill the void of my volunteer work, I do various duties in the church; I joined the church prayer group, sing in the choir and participate in bible study and Sunday school.

Maybe, this is what I was supposed to do, come back to the Mississippi Delta to help some of the peoples that helped me when I was growing up.

Sunday school Trip
to New Orleans

Last year our Sunday school classes went to New Orleans. There were fourteen of us on the trip. We left our homes on Thursday morning, arriving in New Orleans later that day.

On Friday we went to the Aquarium and took a cruise over to the other side, to the Audubon Zoo, the trip was seven miles each way. The Audubon Zoo is internationally acclaimed as one of the top Zoos in the country with over 2,000 of the world's exotic animals including those found in the Louisiana Swamp, which is home to the unique White Alligators displayed in their natural habitats.

On Saturday we went on a Riverboat which featured indoor and outdoor seating space for sightseeing as well as casual dining and cocktail service at the bar on the middle deck and we went to a shopping mall at the Boardwalk.

On Sunday we went to church and then to Six Flags Amusement Park before returning home late Sunday night. We all enjoyed the trip and had a good time.

My Cousin Passes Away

Since I have been back in the Delta, My sister and I visited one of our cousins in Illinois, we stayed with him over the weekend. He was very glad to see us. We cooked and refrigerated several different meals to be warmed up for him after we had left. At ninety eight years old he was still able to live in his house, with someone coming in daily to check on him and to assist in his care. He also had a housekeeper to clean the house. I would call him at least twice a week

The last time that I talk to him was about 3:00 P.M. in the afternoon. He passed away a little after 8:00 P.M. that same day. He was ninety eight years old. I traveled to Illinois by bus to my cousin's funeral. While on the bus I met a young man that sat beside me, he was so polite, he was nineteen years old. He told me that he was on his way to Army Basic Training. I told him about my grandchildren and children that were in the Military. The bus ride from Mississippi to Illinois was long, the bus would stop, so that we could use the rest room, stretch and buy food. I noticed that he didn't have much food or money. I had packed lots of food for my trip. I asked the young man if I would give him a bag of my food, would he accept it, he told me he would. So, I gave it to him along with a bottle of water. Then I asked him if he had any money. He pulled from his side pocket five, $1 bills.

This young man had almost two days more of traveling. I gave him $5 and told him to buy himself a hot sandwich. He told me he would at the next bus stop. The next stop was the point for me to gets-off. But, for the young man it was just another rest stop.

A lady that was on the bus with us, noticed me talking to him. As I got off the bus in Illinois, she asked him if he wanted two sandwiches that she had, he told her that he was all right now. I thank God, that I was at the right place and time, to be able to help this young man. I told him that I hope if one of my children or grandchildren were somewhere and needed help that someone would help them.

While at my cousin funeral I got a chance to meet some of my cousins on my father side that I had never met before, we promised to stay in touch. My cousin has been dead almost a year now. I have called my cousin that assisted in taking care of him. I left a voice message on her answering service. I told her that our cousin wanted us to keep in touch; I asked her to call me, I never heard from her. Two years later I was in Illinois with one of my other cousins and we went by her house, she said that she was glad to see me but I have not heard from her since, I tried to do what my cousin asked. Life had been good to my cousin; he lived to an old age.

Sunday school Trip to Orlando

Our Sunday school classes went to Orlando Florida. There were forty of us including the children. I was looking forward to the trip this year, since we all had so much fun together last year. We had several fund raisings to help us with the expenses. I enjoyed the trip, the weather was fantastic. We stayed at the Hilton Hotel. We were able to do some shopping, go to Magic Kingdom, watched a parade and observed evening fireworks.

This is a happy time for me since I decided to leave the North and come back to the South. The winter weather was getting too hard for me alone to keep the driveway and carport free from snow. I would be outside shoveling snow at 5:00 A.M. in the morning. Some days I would have to shovel twice a day. This was a good decision that I had made, when I decided to move back South. I had hurt my wrist shoveling, and was sometimes in pain. I had been retired for three years. My son and I was the only family member living there, there was no reason to live there now. My job had transferred me there eight years earlier. My family was still living in the city that I was transfer from.

I now live a couple of houses from my niece. She takes care of my house when I am away. I can feel safe traveling, knowing that my sister and niece will take care of my house for me. Now, that I am settled, I would like to travel more. If I had remained here in the south, my life would be different. The South would not have prepared me for the life I now have. I would not have gotten the education that I needed after dropping out of school at an early age. I also had the opportunity to travel to different states and even out of the country.

I was able to get the education that I needed, I have spent most of my adult life in classes. I have had classes at Huntsville College in Huntsville Alabama, Penn-State Behrend College and Erie Business Center in Erie Pennsylvania. I have attended classes in Cleveland and Youngtown Ohio, Pittsburgh and Philadelphia Pennsylvania, Boston Massachusetts and at Air Bases and Army Reserve Centers. I took a computer classes at home where I had to set-up the computer; I did all of my tests on the computer, my grades would be mailed to me. I was able to make all A's and B's. I also took a class on electricity for the residence and I attended classes by going to Vocation Tech Center at night.

God opened doors for me that I didn't even know were there. God has also blessed me to be able to travel to Los Angeles California, Seattle and Tacoma Washington, New Orleans Louisiana, Orlando Florida, Houston Texas, Nashville Tennessee, Washington, DC, North Carolina, South Carolina, Virginia and overseas to London, Mexico and South Africa.

March 31 to April 1, I attended a Women of Faith Conference in Shreveport/Bossier City, Louisiana. I enjoyed this conference very much. There were over ten thousands women there. I can truly say that I have been blessed. I hope that whoever read this would know that they can change their life too.

If you have read this far, it is time that I tell you where I lived. I live in the Mississippi Delta town of Rolling Fork. When I left the Delta, I went to Pennsylvania to the town of Erie. When my job transferred me to a new location, it was to Johnstown Pennsylvania.

Life was not always easy; I had good times and bad times. Studying was very hard, I prayed for God's help all the way. I had six children to care for and I was still very young myself. I was the mother of six children's at the age of twenty-nine.

When my sixth child was born, my mother came to live with me. I started as a young girl from a small town in the Delta with very limited education and became a successful career person, who truly knew where my help came from, doors were opened for me that I didn't even know existed. As long as you know, with God all things are possible. We cannot do anything on our own, we need God.

Now all of my six children; three girls and three boys have grown up, have their own families and still live in the North. My oldest son is still in the military.

My family and I talk on the phone every day. We are a close family, all six of my children's and their families. I also keep in close touch with my sisters and brothers. I talked to my stepsister and niece that live in Los Angeles.

I am also fortunate to have made a close friend that lives in the town that my job transferred me too. We keep in touch by phone and cards.

Over the years my six children and their families have had an annual get together. In 2003 we had our first annual gathering, we gathered in Johnstown Pennsylvania, in 2004 we met at my son's home in Stafford Virginia, in 2005 they returned to Mississippi and I went to Erie to spend Thanksgiving with my family.

In October 2005, I had eye surgery on both of my eyes. While on the bus I became temporarily blind for a few minutes. Right after I got where I could only see a blur, we came to a rest stop. I got off the bus seeing very little, not clear at all. I followed the other passengers into the rest area, after awhile my sight slowly came back. I was praying all the time. I got me a sandwich and went back to the bus. I think my eyes were tired, and needed a rest. When I got back on the bus I closed them for a while. But I kept opening them to make sure I could still see. When I got where I was going, I brought a pair of sunglasses. I think the strain on my eyes was too much, I was supposed to be wearing sunglasses in the bright light. I surely thank God for letting me be able to see again. Now, I wear sunglasses when I am out in the sun.

This year, 2006, by the grace of God my son will be retiring in August with thirty years of active military service. My older daughter husband retired last year in 2005. I have grandchildren in Elementary School, Middle School, High School and College. I also have great grandchildren.

Church Sunday school Trip

In 2006 my church planned a trip to Luverne, Minnesota. There we were supposed to sing at a church. Some of the members of the church in Luverne, Minnesota visit our church every year to teach vacation bible school. We promised them that we would visit them this year.

At 1:30A.M., on June 1ˢᵗ, we started our trip, there were twenty-six of us. Our first stop was at 8:30 A.M. in Jasper Missouri for breakfast, we ate at McDonald. We arrived in Kansas City Missouri at 11:30 A.M. that morning, we had lunch at Applebee. I had Steak, Broccoli, Garlic Mashed Potatoes and a Cherry/Lime Soda. Then we went to the Kansas City Zoo, where we stayed until about 3:00 P.M. then we were able to check into the hotel.

The Hotel was in Overland Park. The next morning we had breakfast at the hotel. They served a very good, hot breakfast. After we finished breakfast, we boarded the bus to go to Sioux Falls South Dakota. We were only a short distance from Kansas City Missouri when a truck driver driving an eighteen wheel truck came across in front of us and hit the front bumper of our bus. It happen so fast, no one even had a chance to scream.

Our driver was very experienced; we really thank God for him. God directed the bus, but used him to steer it, no one was seriously injured. The driver was shaken up and received a slight injury and was taken to the hospital.

After the accident, most of us were sitting on the bus while a few were outside looking around, and then they got back on the bus to wait. About an hour later, a bus came to pick us up to take us to the hotel that the State Trooper had called. It was a bus from a local Baptist Church, the driver was very nice.

When we got to the hotel, off loaded our bags and went to check in we discovered that the hotel only had room for half of our group, the other half would have to stay at another hotel. By this time our driver had been released from the hospital, he was okay; the doctor told him that he would be sore the next day. After the driver was picked up at the hospital, he and one of the ladies found a hotel that could accommodate all of us and the driver and the lady were already at the hotel arranging for our stay. We were able to get an angel posing as a cab driver. The cab driver made six trips between the two hotels with four of us at a time. He would load his trunk and go from one hotel to the other until our entire luggage was at the new hotel where we spent the night.

We got hotel rooms in St. Joseph Missouri; we ate lunch, went to the mall, did some shopping, and returned back to the hotel. The hotel had a swimming pool where the children could swim. Some of our group went over to Red Lobster for dinner. But the ladies that I was sharing a room with, we decided to stay at the hotel and send out for our dinner. We each ordered a salad and we got parsley biscuits to go with it.

Early the next morning a passenger bus and a pickup truck came to pick us up. They called our Mayor and Deacon of our church. They got a father and son to drive the bus. The Mayor and the Deacon drove the truck to pull the trailer back that our luggage was in; the truck belonged to the Mayor. We can only say thank you God for guiding and directing our path. We had no worry;

we knew that God would provide our needs. We had breakfast at Denny the next morning, which was Sunday. Then we loaded the bus for our return trip home. We arrived home at 4:00 A.M. on Monday morning.

Mother's Day

Mother Day at the church was very good. The men of the Church decided to surprise the women with a dinner after the Sunday church service, the men served dinner. In the month of June for Father's Day, the women thought it was a very good idea to do the same for the men. A few women of the Church came up with a surprise for the men. After Sunday church service, we served dinner to the men at the same social center that they had served us. The dinner was for all; the men, women and children of the Church, we also served our visitors. We had a great time, sitting around laughing and talking. Everyone agreed it was a very good get together, we promised that we would do this more often.

On June 19, we started our annual revival. Our speaker was our own young Associate Pastor, he delivers a very spirited message, and we all left the church very uplifted. We are looking forward to the rest of the week. After the revival our Associate Pastor was offered the job as Pastor in a nearby town, he accepted it. A short time later our Pastor got sick and was placed in a nursing home.

Over the last year, our church has been relying on several guest pastors to provide our Sunday service and church members have been conducting the bible studies. After several months we are now in the process selecting a pastor. We had three pastors from different locations provide our church services on second and fourth Sunday. We decided to vote for the one that would be our pastor. For the first vote the pastor with the least votes was eliminated. The next time we had service we voted again and this time the one with the most votes became our pastor. Our pastor is a young man; he and his wife are from a nearby town, we are happy to have them.

Family Spends a Week in Lafayette Indiana

We went on our family week trip to Lafayette Indiana. It was with the family of my cousin on my father's side of the family. I went by bus to the city where my cousin lives, then later that night we all met the others family members at her church. The bus left for Lafayette later that night.

We traveled on a charter bus, where we had lots of room; the seats were wide and spacious. Most family members had their own seat. We stopped for breakfast the next morning; the trip was twelve hours long. We were able to check into the hotel at 3:00 P.M. that day, which was a Saturday. My cousin and I shared a suite for the week.

On Sunday we went to the Tippecanoe Mall and a Flea Market across the street from the hotel, we did lots of shopping. After our shopping spree we all went to Ryan's for dinner. On Monday we went downtown to an Art Museum, that evening we had dinner at Golden Corral. On Tuesday most of our families went to an indoor go-kart track for amusement. The older ones including me decided that go-karts were not for us, that evening we ate dinner at the hotel where we were staying. On Wednesday we went back to the Tippecanoe Mall and that evening had dinner at the hotel where we were staying. Thursday most of our family, at least the younger ones went to the Indiana Beach Amusement Park. They got back to the hotel in time for dinner. Dinner was from 5:00-7:00 P.M. each night.

On Friday, we were all looking forward to a family fun day, full of lots of food. At 11:30 A.M. we all boarded the bus with lots of food and we went to Columbia Park. We took a train ride, which was $1.00. There were over thirty of us that went on the ride. Some of our family members stayed back to prepare the food for us to eat. At 3:00 P.M. we ate, sat around talking, eating and laughing, enjoying our time together.

After eating, family pictures were taken. Each family member's individual photo was also taken. Then a picture was taken of the entire family, this was a day to remember. I was able to get a picture of me with my family on my father's side. Afterwards, we went back to the hotel carrying lots of food for later.

On Saturday, one week from the day that we arrived in Lafayette, we packed to leave for home. We had a few hours to waste before leaving so we checked out of the hotel at 11:00 A.M. and went back to the mall for the last time. We had to manage our time carefully, the time we left the mall was important because we had to arrive at a designated location at a precise time to change bus drivers, the new driver would drive the bus to our destination. We arrived at our destination about 3:00 A.M. in the morning. I spent the night with my cousin, on Sunday we went to Sunday school at my cousin's church, I enjoyed it very much. After it was over, she took me to the bus station. I arrived home later that day.

My Son Retires

It is now the last of July 2006, and we are getting ready to leave on the second of August for my oldest son's thirty year military retirement party in Virginia. We also made it our annual family-get-together. Since my job relocation away from my children, we have made it an annual event for my children and their families to have a gathering. When we have our get together, other family members and friends are always welcome.

On August 4, my oldest son retired from the Marine Corps, the entire family went to Virginia for his retirement, and we celebrated the entire weekend. Twenty-five of us stayed at his home and another twelve family members stayed at the hotel. My oldest daughter and her family brought their camper and stayed in it in his backyard. My middle daughter also stayed in the camper with them. The camper had two-queen size beds inside, one on each end. That Thursday evening, we had Smoked Turkey, Brisket, Salads, Dip and Chip. We had a good time greeting and reminiscing.

On Friday morning we had to be ready to leave the house at 8:30 A.M. The retirement ceremony was going to start at 10:00 A.M. For breakfast we had donuts, bagels, cereal, coffee, juice and tea. We attended my son's retirement. After the retirement was over, we went to the Officer's Club for lunch. At the ceremony and luncheon there were ninety-three peoples in attendance. The food was good; we had several varieties on the menu, it was served buffet style. We could eat as much as we wanted too. We had a good time and there was lots of food and friends. Later that afternoon we went back to the house, that evening we had a fish fry, fried okra, macaroni & cheese, hush puppies, and corn on the cob.

Saturday morning breakfast consisted of donuts, bagels, cereal, coffee, juice and tea. For lunch we had hot dogs, hamburgers and Coleslaw. Later that afternoon they went to pick up the pig for the pig roast we had planned for later that day. The pig was washed and seasoned; the coal placed in the container that the pig was going to be roasted in was getting hot. The pig was put into the container; every thirty minute they added more charcoal. When the pig was almost done, they had to remove the ashes from the container cover so that the pig could finish browning inside the container. We were all excited to see the finished product. It turned out to be perfect, the skin golden brown, and it only took only four-and-a-half hours from start to finish. My youngest son fried two turkeys. My middle daughter and I made dirty rice, Jambalaya with sausage and shrimp, we also made a Green Bean Casserole with French Beans, baked beans and we had shrimp on the stick. For desert, I had prepared seven cakes; three, Sock-it- to-me Cakes, three, Friendship Cakes along with a large Coconut Pound Cake.

Sunday morning we had a light breakfast and fruit salad. Most everyone was leaving for home. There were lots of leftovers. Almost everyone carried some kind of food with them when they left for home.

My only regret, my daughter in law and her family and my family were all together at one time, and we forgot to take pictures of the individual family members along with a group photo of both families together.

The last of the family left late that night, leaving my friend and me. We stayed back to help my son and his wife clean their house. We stayed through Tuesday morning, leaving just before day light, my son and grandson returned to Mississippi with me, they would fly back home in ten days. We arrived in Mississippi late Tuesday evening.

On Wednesday we got up early and cut the grass and spent the remainder of the days unpacking, resting and enjoying each other's company. Thursday, we had odd and end jobs to do. Friday we went to Jackson, approximately two hours away to the Airport to pick up my granddaughter. It was her first time visiting Mississippi since she was about eleven years old.

We all spent the week just relaxing. We cooked different southern dishes, so my granddaughter would get a taste of southern cooking as well as learn to make a few dishes. By the time she left for home, we had baked three cakes, including a 7-Up Cake.

At 2:45 A.M. the next Friday, my friend, son and my two grandchildren left. My friend was going by his home in southern Mississippi to visit his family for a few days. My son and grandson were flying back to Virginia and my granddaughter was flying back to North Carolina. They were all going in different directions. I thank God they all arrived home safely.

My Family

It is now 2007, and, if God is willing, we will be having our Family Reunion in Vicksburg Mississippi. Our family reunion planning is going great, we are hearing from cousins on my grandmother side of the family. After this reunion, I think that I will retire from the responsibility of planning and organizing the reunions and ensuring that everything is being done. I have truly enjoyed it, but the work is getting too hard for me. We are turning it over to the younger generation.

In April my youngest daughter and son came to visit me for a week, I was very glad to have them. Nothing is like having your children with you, if it is only for a visit. We know that all good things have to come to an end; they had to go back to their families.

In May, I had been back living in the Mississippi Delta three years. I may have moved to the South for the weather. But I was able to help look after my father-in-law. His wife had passed away, he couldn't take care of himself any longer and my brother-in-law was not able to take care of him. His son had put him in a nursing home in our town. My brother-in-law was the husband of my older sister, and the brother of my ex-husband. My sister passed away in 1993.

I would visit my father-in-law and take him little snacks that he likes to eat. I would also dial my ex-husband, his son, on my cell phone, so, he would be able to talk to his son. This continued until he passed away about a week before his ninety-fourth birthday. Now, my brother-law is sick, he has been sick for some time. Now, I am here to help him as much as I can. He knows that he can call me anytime.

My cousin that lives in Tennessee is ninety-four years old. I call him regularly to see how he is getting along. He is the now the oldest in our family.

I am enjoying my retirement in the Delta. The only thing is that the weather sometime can be frightening. Sometimes there are severe thunder storm and tornado warning all night accompanied with heavy rain, thundering and lighting. After it is over, we thank God that it has passed us by again.

I still have lots of flowers that I take care of. I keep them inside during the winter. But during the summer I have even more flowers to care for inside and outside. I also keep up my yard, by cutting my own grass.

Our family reunion was a success; lots of our family members were there. We had a DJ and lots of food. From Saturday night to Monday evening there was never a dull moment, we were all excited to see each other. The younger children enjoyed the moon bouncer. My cousin that lived in Tennessee was in the hospital during our planning stage. We prayed that he would be able to attend. But it was not God's will; he passed away at ninety four years old.

Following the Family Reunion, our Fourth of July cookout with all of my children's and grandchildren was held at my house. Five of my children and their families were able to make it. I was sorry that my baby girl was not able to come. There were seventeen of us, my older daughter and her family stayed at my sister's house with fourteen staying at my house. For our sleeping arrangement, we had blowup mattresses everywhere. My children were able to stay for a week; they have a very good friend that grew up with them from about five or six years old, he is now considered a part of the family, for the last three years he has been attending our get together.

On July third we had a fish fry, on the fourth of July we had a cookout, and Wednesday and Thursday we went to Greenville to shop. Thursday evening we had a fish fry, everyone enjoyed themselves. My oldest son and his family left on Wednesday going back to Virginia, my middle son and some of his cousins left on Friday morning, my friend from Pennsylvania also left on Friday morning. The rest of my family stayed on until Saturday morning.

A few months ago, one of my cousins that lived in Michigan gave his sister my e-mail address; she emailed me the next day. After that I called her, she told me about my uncle's children who was my mother's brother. They live in California where she lives. She gave me their phone numbers; one of my cousins lives here in Mississippi. I was so happy; I called them both the same day. My cousin in Mississippi and my cousin that lives in California, we haven't talked to each other since we were kids. Our parents were living, now they are gone, we promised to stay in touch.

This morning one of my cousins emailed me to tell me that one of my cousins that lives in Jackson Mississippi wife passed away yesterday with a heart attack, I called him right away. I haven't talk to him since my older sister passed away years ago.

All my cousins are getting together again, for the home going of my cousin's wife. We promise to get together again without it being a sad occasion. God has been truly good to our family.

It is now almost the end of 2007. There has been quite a change in my life. One of my granddaughters is having her second child; she is expecting a girl this time. Her other child is a two year old boy. They tell me that another one of my granddaughters is having a baby; she has a little boy already. My long time friend has moved to Mississippi now to stay. We are enjoying going to movies and taking three miles walks together. He is enjoying riding the bicycle when the weather is nice,

67

which is most of the times. My sister and I walk two miles on Monday and Thursday, we enjoy our talks while we walk.

We are already talking about our get together with my children, their families and whatever friends that wants to come next year. If God is willing, we will be going to Virginia. We look forward to our get together once a year. This is a time for us all to enjoy each other company without it being a sad occasion. God had blessed us for quite a few years to do this. We started our annual family gatherings in Johnstown Pennsylvania after my job relocation. Now, the family looks forward to it.

I have enjoyed moving back to the Delta after being away so long. When I call my family up North, and they tell me that it is snowing, I thank God that I am in a nice warm climate with no snow.

After living here for five years, I am still singing in the choir, going to Sunday school and attending Bible Study on Wednesday Nights. I am still active around the house inside and out and I still take care of all my flowers.

My nephew passed away this year he lived in Lansing Michigan. My sister and I caught the bus to Erie; my son came from his home in Virginia to take us to Lansing to the funeral. We arrived at the hotel at 12:30 A.M. on Friday Morning. We were about thirty miles from Lansing. The funeral was at 12:00 noon on Friday. We left early on Friday morning for Lansing, where we went to one of our family member's home. The funeral was very sad; lots of family and friends from all around were there. On Saturday my son returned us to Erie and left early Sunday morning for home. My sister left by bus later that day, I stayed on for a week, and then I returned home. My friend drove me home; it was a lot better than riding the bus. I really enjoyed being with my children and grandchildren.

It is now the end of 2008, life has been good to me. I am still enjoying walking three miles, three times a week. My family and I had our get together in August. This year, we all went to Virginia. God has truly blessed us all; we were able to make it. We had lots of fun just being together. A few weeks later most of the children went to visit their father in Michigan.

One of my cousins that live in Chicago has been put in a nursing home, and one that lives in California has passed away. Also, one of my cousins' sons was killed; he was shot three times by his wife. We know that this is God's will and he want put any more on us than we can bear.

It is 2010; we no longer have our senior choir at church. The young folks are doing all the singing. I am thinking of going on the mother board. We only have three mother of the church. The oldest one's health is not too good, maybe I can help.

In mid 2010, I joined the mother's board. I have been on the board for several months now. If God is willing I am getting ready to go on a cruise in September of this year. I will be going to Mexico with friends. I can still say God has truly blessed me.

Well, it's now September 2010, and I did go on my five-day trip to Mexico. There were twenty of us in my group. The cruise ship made two stops in Mexico. We boarded the ship at about 1:00 P.M. on Saturday afternoon and set sail, Sunday was a Fun Day at Sea.

On Monday, we had our first stop in Progreso Mexico. We were there from 7:00 A.M. to 4:00 P.M. Tuesday was our second stop in Cozumel Mexico. We were there from 9:00 A.M. until 5:00 P.M. While there we did lots of shopping for souvenirs for our family and friends. We also did a lot of eating, I enjoyed myself. This is another one of my trips that I would love for my family to take.

It is the last day of summer now. I have traveled a lot this year. It is now time for me to stay home and get ready for the winter weather.

When Challenged Keep Going

I have said to my children over the years, you probably don't know much about my life. What I have been through and where God has taken me too. I want them to know that, I have done things and went places, that only God could take me too. As long as you have faith and believe, the sky is the limit.

I decided to put my life into writing, as much as I could. I asked a lady I knew how I could get started; she had done this before, so I knew she could tell me. She was in the process of writing her life story. She asked me about mine, I told her some of it, and then she said; wait until God tell you to do it. Then you will find someone to publish it for you. I realized at that moment that she was not going to tell me anything. Perhaps my life stories seem like a threat to her. We live only a short distance from each other and she didn't want mine to interfere before hers came out. I learned a lot that night by talking to her; she was not interested in telling me how to get started. She was only trying her best to do everything for herself, but not willing to help anyone else. She couldn't see inside my heart like God, only the outside. How did she know that God wasn't in the plan all along, she may have been the person that I was supposed to ask for the information. But she refused; she may have missed her blessing.

God has been in everything that I have tried to do. What God have for me, no one can take it. It is only for me and what God has for her, no one can take it. She could have answered my question; it would not have hurt her chances at all. Peoples may seem interested in what you do, but when they think that it will somehow interfere with their plans, they don't want to help you. Be prepared to accept peoples not helping you on most things you do. Even if they are asked, sometime they may think that you are not ready to continue with your plan. If God is in the plan, you will get it anyway.

God has opened doors for me, that some of my family and friends will never believe. I know that some thought that I got married too early in age, having six children by the time I was twenty nine years old was not very smart, and that I would never amount to anything. But God knew all along what he had in store for me. The plan was all his, I just had to have faith and believe that I could do it. I have worked all day, and went to school at night. I have gotten laid off from my job, and worked two part-time jobs. This didn't stop me from going to school and trying my best to learn more. Keep on asking and it will be given to you, keep on seeking and you will find, keep on knocking and the door will be opened to you. Writing this has truly been a blessing in my life. I hope that it will not only help my children, grandchildren and great grandchildren one day, but everyone that read it, with God in your life nothing is impossible.

Conclusion

If you have read this far, I hope that you have enjoyed it. You see that my family and I had good times and bad times. But we all have truly been blessed. We thank God for everything. None of this would have been possible without God in our lives. Whatever you go thru in life, there is always someone else worst off than you are. We all have choices to make in life. With our choices, we try not to make the wrong ones. Let us concentrate on getting it right if we are given a second change.

The End

About the Author

This is written from my experience. I had six children before I was twenty-nine years old. I was living in the south at a time when opportunities were few because of my limited education; and, not knowing what to do next. Today, I can say that I overcame my circumstance to become the person I am today. I have had lots of education from different schools and colleges. I was a Mechanical Inspector for an Aerospace Corporation and I was a Quality Assurance Specialist for the Federal Government. I have been a volunteer at the local hospital, treasurer, and chairperson for press and publicity for an organization. I am back living in the Mississippi Delta. I am a retired government employee. I have been places and seen things that only God could bless me with. There is nothing wrong with living in the South, it was the education that I needed and was able to get. There is nothing to impossible for God, keep the faith.

This book is about a young girl growing up in the Mississippi Delta, it tells of the struggles of her parents. She realizes at an early age that she needs a better education in order to have a better life. She wants her children to have things that she didn't. She decides to go back to school to better her-self; it takes hard work and many years to get to her goal. She has to work during the day and go to school at night. She would walk long distances to get to work and sometimes had to work two jobs. There were countless stumbling blocks put in her life, sometime it seem impossible. There were people that tried to give her doubt by telling her that she couldn't do such things. The book tells you that you can do what you want in life, you have choices and how she was able to overcome it all.